JEWEL DROPPER

BY: SHEENA JOHNSON

Sheena Johnson   Jewel Dropper

Copyright 2021, Sheena Johnson

ISBN: 978-1-7356518-0-4

All Rights Reserved. No part of this book may be reproduced or transmitted in any form or by any means, electronic or mechanical, including photo-copyright, recording, or by any information storage and retrieval system without written permission from the author except for the inclusion of brief quotations in a review.

Printed in the United States of America.

Jewel Dropper

Table of Content

Ambition..7-8

Where I'm From.......................................9-10

Five Senses...11-13

Struggles..14-15

Lost of HipHop.......................................16-17

Hood Life...18

Gemini Vibe...19-20

Random Drug Test..................................21-22

Elimination...23-24

Outspoken...25-26

Goodbye..27-29

Rescue...30-31

Down and Dirty......................................32

Funny Styles..33-34

American Gangster.................................35-36

Realness Dead or Alive............................37

Five Seconds……………………………………………38-40

No Signs of Commitment……………………………41-42

Shine………………………………………………………43

Morning Prayer…………………………………………44

My Sisters…………………………………………………45-46

Runners……………………………………………47

Hood Anthem…………………………………….48-50

Real Ones………………………………………….51-52

The Cage…………………………………………..53-55

Exposure…………………………………………..56

Katrina……………………………………………..57-58

Fly Girl……………………………………………..59

Resume'……………………………………………60-61

Signing Off………………………………………..62-63

Don't Wanna Sell Crack………………………64-65

3rd Eye……………………………………………..66-67

Lost Baby Mom…………………………………68

Knock Off the User……………………………69

After the Storm………………………………..70

Wise Guide……………………………………….71

Employee	72-73
Never Neglect Yourself	74-75
Stopped Looking	76-77
Joy	78
Dream Lover	79
Can I Comfort You	80-81
Brainwashed	82-83
Over	84
Closed Curtains	85
Changing Lanes	86-87
Canceled Program	88-89
The Flipside	90
My Mother's Child	91
Jezebel	92-93
Camelot Troy	94-95
Quran Geter	96-97
I Need Growth	98
Being Set Free	99
A Monster Without a Face	100-101
Janyll	102-103

Signals……………………………………………………104-105

Never Make It More……………………………………106-107

The Way He Loves Me…………………………………108

Cardiac Care………………………………………………109

Dope Dick…………………………………………………110

Closure………………………………………………………111-112

I'm Up…………………………………………………………113-114

Turn The Tables…………………………………………115

Don't Rush Life……………………………………………116

Long Distance Lover……………………………………117-118

Halfway House Resident……………………………119-120

The Pussy Chase…………………………………………121-122

The Good Die Young………………….123-124

Jewels……………….125

Icy Cold Word…………………….126-127

Sheena Johnson · Jewel Dropper

Ambition

My blood is black, my complexion is beige

I never changed

Just a few things been rearranged

My body's getting thicker

My pockets a little bigger,

I'm a lover not a fighter

But never afraid to knuckle up or pull a trigger

Often respond to Digga while others call me Sheena

I got that Snapper that pours that pure Aquafina

I got that "Fire and Desire" like Rick James and Teena

Your sixth sense, is your common sense

That'll have you spending dollars instead cents

I'm on the road to riches with real Bitches like Ms. Wentz

If you're on the run keep running

If you're a Hustler Hustling keep hugging

Sheena Johnson   Jewel Dropper

We eat that cheesy bread that Bakers can't bake in the oven

We boil loafs on the stove

Puffing reefer sipping Remy listening to Hov

The Hustlers are getting younger and so are The Hoes

I suppose, I gotta stay on my toes

No snitching no telling no confession

If you get caught with cocaine in your possession

Just take it as a lesson

Do your time and next time pay attention
Born and raised in CMD, New Jersey where shit get real

Fairview, Parkside, Downtown, Cramer Hill

North Camden, East Camden, Polock and The Vill

I was born and raised in Polock the home of The Hill

I am a Beast

Straight from the Streets

That's tryna Harvest something more than a feast

I do it for Wadiyah, my Mother and my Niece

And for my Brother that's locked down and for Janyll Brittany Latrice continue resting in Peace

Sheena Johnson   Jewel Dropper

Where I'm From

Where I'm from, you'll see a bird or a plane when u look up to the sky

Along with a pair of sneakers on the electrical wire hanging high

Milk crates used as basketball courts and for seats leaving prints on the back side of your thighs

Children wandering the streets after midnight on a school night

You're liable to see a young boy letting off bullets in broad daylight

These young boys now days are bold

Their hearts must be made of steel that's freezing cold

The drive by and face mask strategy to these young boys is old

They'll walk straight up to you and bang you, for the right price your soul gets sold

A lot of people confused, lost and ruthless

Domestic violence, bad hygiene and drugs has many people toothless

Whenever a girl is book smart and street smart she's considered exclusive

All the dope boys look at her as good usage

Sheena Johnson — Jewel Dropper

Hustlers cook up meals made of baking soda

A strong substance that carries a heavy odor

Fiends used to be "The Shit" but fucked up as they got older

Their used to be flawless face now has more acne than acid has in soda

Grandparents become grandparents before reaching age thirty

Little young girls out here contracting Aids and Herpes

From lying down with a older Man who's dick was dirty

This shit is happening everywhere not just in Camden, New Jersey

However, let's get one thing understood

You're not from the streets if you're not from the hood

Never rep the urban inner cities if you were raised good in the suburbs or the woods

To claim you were raised in the struggle will never do you any good

This is for the fiend with the lean and the blood shot eyes

Who stopped chasing their dreams to run after the high

I do it for the realest prisoners doing bids and for the kids that are unsupervised

Last but not least, for everyone in the struggle worldwide

Especially the real niggas that lost their lives

Sheena Johnson   Jewel Dropper

Five Senses

I saw a lot of shit with my vision

I saw a pregnant chick sniffing Dope, two cars crash in a collision

I saw a man get murdered but I act like I was blind

So, when they ask for witnesses and suspects, I'm not the one they wanna find

I saw a rainbow in my life once or twice

I saw a pretty Boy get stuck up for his ice

I saw a Nigga driving around in foreign cars with stars

Having pretty Bitches stripping, drinking expensive liquor in bars

I watched them Men ball

Five years later, a rat snitched, caused the empire to fall

I saw hundreds of my family & friends in a casket looking like their sleep

I saw someone who didn't keep a secret they were suppose to keep

That's some of what I saw now this is what I felt

I felt pressure when the cherry got popped under my belt

I felt a lot of emotional and physical pain

Sheena Johnson   Jewel Dropper

I felt Carl Thomas's Emotional & Summer Rain

I felt 21 tattoos

I've been hurt by both real and wack ass dudes

I felt a white owl and a dutch

It's over when my phalanges and a ink pen touch

I felt contractions in my back and lower abdominal area while I was in labor

Losing a baby due to a miscarriage is more painful then getting cut by a knife or razor

That's some of what I felt now this what I tasted

I tasted mace when I got sprayed in the face

I tasted Purple Haze

The shit that'll leave u amazed

I tasted milk from a farm

I tasted Coronas, Smirnoff, 211's and Boone's Farm

I tasted the lips of a Sinner

I tasted TV Dinners

I tasted a soda that under the cap read "sorry you're not a winner"

That's some of what I've tasted now this is what I heard

I heard Christians call the Holy Bible "The Word"

Sheena Johnson   Jewel Dropper

I heard my name in he say, she say

I heard Nas and Wale

Are amongst The Greatest poets of my day

I heard it takes a second to die but a minute to pray

I heard Beanie Siegel's The Truth

I learned a lot from The Late Great Dr. Ruth

I heard when a Nigga fucks more than one Bitch he's a Pimp for sure

I heard when a Bitch fucks more than one Nigga she's a fucking whore

That's some of what I heard now this is what I smelled

Growing up, on the first of the month I smelled money through the mail

I smelled somebody smoking a laced L

I smelled The Cooker cooking Coke

I smelled the smell of gun smoke

I smelled sex on the beach incense

Common sense is your sixth sense

Sheena Johnson　　　　　　　　　　　　　　　　　　Jewel Dropper

Struggle

Tell me what your life like, I'm strictly from the gutter

Slept on a twin size mattress with my Brother and my Mother

Cooking with lard because it wasn't no oil or butter

What you know about getting down on your knees

Not to suck dick but to wash out underwear, bras, socks & jeans

No washer machine so, I gotta wash everything out by hand

No dryer so, I gotta hang everything up by the fan

Eating block cheese and peanut butter that came in a can

What you know about the free meals down at the church

The hunger pains that hurt

Safety pins holding the holes on your shirts

Holes through your clothes bit through by the mouse

When it was no electricity candles lit up the house

No tissue on the roll after you just relief your bowels

The small cash and food stamps was never enough

Times were rough

How can I not be tough

I've been through it all and saw all kinds of stuff

Sheena Johnson   Jewel Dropper

I put a million miles on my feet

Through the hell, rain, snow and the sleet

I froze in the coldest winters and melted through the heat

This little red is riding hood yes, I'm hood I'll scream it loud

I'm hood Black and I'm proud

Can't keep my face out the cloud

Pray to the Gods in the sky

Form clouds when I'm high

Been through so much hurt and pain I can no longer cry

Jealousy, envy and hate makes the crime rate increase

I'm a survivor and a hustler until the day I'm deceased

And to Janyll Brittany Latrice continue resting in the peace

Sheena Johnson Jewel Dropper

Lost of Hip Hop

I wonder if BIG was alive

Would he had come out with a "One More Chance" part two and blow up like the one in 95'

"Juicy" would've became sweeter is what I strongly believe

Would he have made a feature with Nicki, Remy, Drake, Lil Durk, Moneybagg and Eve

Every time he gained a pound

His flows gained a greater sound

It a shame he's no longer around

He's a lost that can never be found

How can a person kill

A Man that was live & real his lyric was ill

Others tried to put on BIGGIE shoes but they never fit

No one can ever spit the way Big spit

The way he came out with hit after hit

BIG is someone who will always be missed

He gets the upmost respect from Nas, Jay-Z & Jada Kiss

It's such a shame how they took the King of Hip Hop

Sheena Johnson   Jewel Dropper

Before they got Biggie they took Tupac

September 96' is when Tupac's life came to an end

When he was just telling us about him and his girlfriend

This Man said "All Eyez on Me"

Because he never had any privacy

With the media following him to his home

With flashing cameras and numbers on microphones

Why did they kill Pac is what I don't know

Is it because he was intelligent, Black with heavy doe

Every time he said a rhyme

His baldhead and nose ring used to always shine

I guess it was Biggie and Tupac's time

Many talented people out here but they were one of a kind

Why did they go is something we'll never know

But in the game of Hip Hop they'll forever be rated number uno

Sheena Johnson Jewel Dropper

Hood Life

Dead broke since birth

The hood's curse

Every day it gets worst

Numb to the pain, it no longer hurts

When those bullets start to burst

Can't be rescue by your Mom, Pop, Doctor or Nurse

Funeral time is the only time you'll see the Young Boys flooded at the church

Not to pray but to carry the coffin and follow the hearse

These streets are stronger than Mexican Tequila straight with no chaser

Home invasions being performed by your next door neighbor

When yesterday you just did them a favor by letting them barrow some toilet paper

Niggas are doing anything for that green piece of paper

In this recession, every profession stressing except the undertaker

Sheena Johnson Jewel Dropper

Gemini Vibe

Bipolar zodiac sign of a Gemini

It's the Thuggish Ruggish Bone in her zone so, please don't blow my high

If so, you'll slaughter the vibe

I'm trying to keep hope alive

But how can I keep hope alive when hope has already died

Thug Life running through my veins Yeahy, Yeahy

Life in the hood is a horror, female fiends reflecting Freddy

Burnt out chasing The Ready

The only element which keeps her steady

She'll take a shake bag or a solid rock as long as the plastic isn't empty

If your money is shaking like it's nervous, you gets no service from the D-Boy

Don't come to the block tryna cop with a pocket full of coins

Cash in your pennies for some dollars and kill that noise

The world is getting deeper than a male teenager voice

I don't care about what you heard, what you saw or what you read

Sheena Johnson   Jewel Dropper

Hip Hop is not dead nor is it misled

It's a culture based on more than new sneakers and new threads

A lot of knowledge spread that'll help you get ahead

In life, your responsible for your own actions enough said

Sheena Johnson   Jewel Dropper

Random Drug Test

A full year, urine clean

Clear eyes no Visine

It's a difficult task when you're a pot head Queen

Desperately in need of the purple and green

I love God and love smoking weed truth be told

My right of smoking Bud is restricted as if I'm on parole

My job performs random drug screenings so I can't get stone

My occupation is my lively hood that keeps the bills paid in my home

Most times I wanna say "fuck this shit" and take a few hits

But if I gamble with the risk

The next morning they might ask for my piss

Fucking with this random shit you'll never know who's next on the list

I must be responsible but this responsibility is a fucked up experience

Being forced to stop, detox and drop the habit of smoking the cannabis

When I light up the weed my soul instantly lifts

Sheena Johnson   Jewel Dropper

What's even worst is that the job ain't getting me rich

Alcoholics coming to work with their pores smelling like liquor

Some coworkers smoke coke because the cocaine comes out their system quicker

The only high I've ever been on is the weed and without her I'm bitter

Next time I'm able to smoke I'm uh light a blunt thicker than a Snicker

Sheena Johnson   Jewel Dropper

Elimination

Can't keep living this life that I'm living

So, today I chose to make a decision

To dig deep inside myself like an incision

Eliminate all who hate, you know the ones who are fiction

Must eliminate the unfaithful mate

I'm too real to deal with the unofficial, artificial and fake

Blessing Blocker blocking me from catching my Big Break

I gotta leave him alone in order to be "Successful" like Trey and Drake

Family is supposed to stick together like paste

Blood thicker than water not true in every case

Blood clots water flows, some family will cross you before your Ace

Only showing love so they eat, sleep and shit in your place

The underdog is on top so, to all those waiting for me drop keep waiting

Many anticipating on the sideline hating

Being brainwashed and used by Satan

Sheena Johnson   Jewel Dropper

This hate shit can make a childhood friend become an old acquaint

Pity parties are the gatherings I never attend

The guests and host are always losers with no desire to win

Misery loves company so be careful who's circle you're in

Jada Kiss told us to keep the grass cut, this is why I keep my circle thin

Sheena Johnson — Jewel Dropper

Outspoken

I'll rather hang with a real nigga that wears weaves and lip gloss like a Bitch

But never will I ever hang with a faggot ass nigga who snitch

Behind walls niggas get soft when taking in for questioning

Spitting shit that they shouldn't even be mentioning

Death before dishonor builds strength and motivation for the heart

Dedication and discipline always plays a major part

Streets are watching, niggas are flipping while others are flopping

No disrespect but it's always cause and effect when pistols are popping

Rejected and misunderstood

All because I'm black and from the hood

Did a few years in College for extra knowledge and they still think I'm up to no good

Previously, I've burnt bridges through bad decisions

Of fucking with these fake ass Niggas and Bitches but now I'm on my mission

Sheena Johnson					Jewel Dropper

I'm determined to create reality for my dreams and visions

Sheena Johnson　　　　　　　　　　　　　Jewel Dropper

Goodbye

You was like my Ace

I never let another park in your space

Took my virginity in the lips when I let you fuck in my face

I provided the greatest pussy

Tight, right and gushy

Wet, fat not bushy

At times when you came the puss was too good for you to push me

We laid up through the snow, heat and the rain

Making love off of Trey Songz driving each other insane

The middle finger is pointed at you, your who I blame

A nigga that's lame

It's a shame

I was your realest Bitch

Jumped in with you when you fell deep in the ditch

I should've listened to my Mom when she said you wasn't shit

How could you fuck around

Thinking it wasn't gonna get back around

Sheena Johnson   Jewel Dropper

I thought my love was found

All along I was just a rebound

No more making plans

Keep satisfying your fans

You're a lying ass Man that keep your dick in your pants

You fucked up forever

You're the reason why we can't stay together

I said I'll never leave you but now I know to never say never

This broken heart will get better

Immediately following this letter

Instead of hugging me, go hug the block and earn so more Cheddar

I'm a girl that's Classy, Sweet, Real & Sassy

There's a Man out there who would love to have me

I loved you from the bottom all the way to the top

Thought you were gonna be at the altar waiting for me and my Pop

It's fucked up how good things come to a stop

Constantly telling me lies

Some nights I silently cried

We can't make it no matter how hard I tried

Sheena Johnson												Jewel Dropper

I never put another above you because I loved you but now I'm saying Goodbye

Rescue

The way that you love me is hotter than the fire from hell

You made me rise when I fell

Before you, I was suffocating waiting to exhale

You're fresh air into the atmosphere, I now breathe easy

I get aroused whenever you touch me and tease me

There's not enough vocabulary in the dictionary to define how you please me

I enjoy the seduction when I'm being seduced

Since you arrived in my life all the pain has reduced

You take me on a high as if I puff a blunt or sipped on The Goose

You hot, brown and sweet like chocolate coco

This love has me insane think I'm going loco

If your love was a brand then I'll sport and support the logo

You're All I Need like Method Man and Mary

I had a vision of love like Mariah Carey

And it was all that you've given to me, it's kind of scary

You're sharper than a machete, blade, sword or a knife

Sheena Johnson   Jewel Dropper

You were once a dream but now your reality into my life

Proved the best things in life aren't attached with a price

Sheena Johnson / Jewel Dropper

Down and Dirty

If I give you some

Will it be a hit and run

Impossible, the way I fuck and use this tongue

You'll be pulling muscles taking deeps breathes through each lung

What I'm saying is Non Fictional

I'll give you more positions than cable has channel on digital

The split that spits between my legs is original

Come see me in 3D, let's get down and dirty

Show me how you can work me

Keeping it strictly physical not emotional so there's no way you'll hurt me

Real is Real

Come touch and feel

My natural juices as they spill

I'm wondering if you're Caddy

Has a gangsta lean that's long enough to make me call u Daddy

If so, wrap it up with a rubber and come grab me

Sheena Johnson   Jewel Dropper

Funny Styles

I've been through some hard times

The proof displays itself on my scar lines

Not eating and sleeping properly because I'm out here on a hard grind

Nobody's giving out handouts so, I gotta go take mines

The devil on my shoulder with temptation which looks like the grand prize

On the opposite angle there's an Angel telling me to go and get baptized

I must stay focus can't slip on a back slide

"Alone in The Streets" Me, Myself and I

The Creator is my only lifeline

I'm dying to live while so many are living to die

In these streets, there's a lot of tricks with no treats, life is one hell of a ride

Merging in and out the lanes of pain just tryna get by

The best way to kill negativity is by being a positive vibe

When you murder bad energy, you're never convicted of the crime

Sheena Johnson   Jewel Dropper

When you come across someone loyal, cherish them because loyalty is hard to find

I'm an old head but older heads claim I'm in my prime

I'm just staying focus and serving my purpose until the end of my earthly time

Sheena Johnson   Jewel Dropper

American Gangsta

I fell in love with Mr. Casanova

A Gangster who will rob and kill to feed his family's hunger

Taught me how to properly clean, unload and load the burner

Taught me education was beauty so, I strived to be a higher learner

Inside his head resides a wizard who's a genius

Embedded in his cranium and inside of his penis

He slings that pipe so right makes me want to carry his fetus

Sike, gotta keep that trojan tight because I'm not the only woman he pleases

He's a Ghetto Super Star

That stays on his radar

Respected and accepted in any hood or any bar

Always keeps a Bad Bitch on his arm

His loyalty and spiritual connection protects him from harm

He said a real woman is never sleazy, she's respectful, classy and calm

Just because I was a Rider he was a provider, telling me to stack the earned income from my job

Sheena Johnson   Jewel Dropper

As he keeps the money flowing through my palm

He's my Homie Lover Friend who can never meet my Mom

Sheena Johnson   Jewel Dropper

Realness Dead or Alive

Young girls out here thotting

Stick up boys plotting

Pistols constantly popping

Bodies constantly dropping

To all the loyal ones who are deceased, you're never forgotten

I'll throw a parade for every Coward that got sprayed

I'll even spit on your grave

Only deal with the real, let me burn on this Haze

Discovery sheets filled with names of lames

It's supposed to be sold and not told when it comes to the game

Striking against The Team is a low blow

Now a days your best bet is to ride solo

You can fall under the category of a youngin, old head, dope head, butch bitch or a Homo

As long as you're real I fuck with you I ain't here to judge you

Sheena Johnson   Jewel Dropper

Five Seconds

When you're in your room all alone

Thinking that nothing is going on you're wrong

Someone is getting weak while someone else is growing strong

Someone is transporting drugs, breaking the law

Some Nigga is about to get burnt for fucking a dirty Bitch raw

So much shit is going down

A fifth grader just brought a bag of weed and a white owl

Someone just collided in a car crash

Some chick is in the mirror putting on her eye lash

Another chick stacking her cash to purchase a new ass

A Junior High School student skipping class

A pimp just slapped his whore

A married man who cheated on his wife is being thrown out the door

A panhandling Bum is singing and dancing with a rich spirit although he's poor

Countries are preparing for war

A female is drinking cranberry juice

Sheena Johnson   Jewel Dropper

So her menstrual cramps can get loose

A small child just lost their first tooth

A family is being evicted for not paying their bill

A senior citizen is ill

Someone is in a financial crisis asking God to take the wheel

A woman just received a diamond she just got engaged

Another woman just posted a post, "Pray for my man he just got shot with a Gage"

There's a billion black men behind bars trapped in a cage

A lame dude is about to snatch some woman's purse

A female is in labor contracting about to give birth

An intern is observing the skills of a doctor and nurse

A man's flesh is about to depart from this earth

Someone's Loving

Someone's Bugging

Someone's Cursing

Someone's Fucking

Someone owes someone money that their ducking

Someone's at a knife fight about to receive a lifetime scar

Another person is auditioning to be a star

Sheena Johnson   Jewel Dropper

Some old man is getting drunk in a bar

Someone is selling Moonshine out of a mason jar

Less than five seconds all this shit went on

The shit will keep happening even when you're gone

Sheena Johnson Jewel Dropper

No Signs of Commitment

Everyone needs someone to Love; Love is an emotional source that's suppose to bring out the best in you

But what do you do when you've giving your all, to the point you feel as if emptiness is the only thing left in you

Love ain't Love if all it does is constantly depressing and stressing you

We all go through trials and tribulations, I guess this is just God's way of testing you

No hugs or kisses there's truly something missing

When I try giving you my Love you instantly become resistant

Labeled me as your woman however, I don't feel a dedicated quality of commitment

Claim that there's no other woman but intuition tells me different

You play "The Blame Game" claiming everything's my fault

All I ever wanted was to illuminate light to your life with an luminous volt

I've satisfactorily completed the requirements for faithfully loving you so remember my loyalty as you walk

Although I love you, there will be no forms of communication, when it's over it's over, I'm not the type to stalk

Sheena Johnson   Jewel Dropper

Another lesson learned and another lesson taught

Sheena Johnson   Jewel Dropper

Shine

Like a full moon floating through jet black skies

She shines

Miss independent with those Ebony eyes

This girl is magical

She'll give you butterflies inside of your abdominal

A wonderful phenomenal woman beautiful and spiritual

When she walks she struts like a model

She leads and never follows

Naturally built like a classic coke bottle

An earthly goddess who got it honest, this girl is flawless

Hotter than the month of August

She's every Man's dream

Her shoe game is mean

Whenever she's seen

She's always put well together and clean

She on top of her game like a ceiling

An open mind who's brilliant

Like the late great Aaliyah this girl is One in a million

Sheena Johnson   Jewel Dropper

Morning Prayer

Creator, thanks for waking me up this morning to see another day

I ask that you lead and guide me every step of the way

Give me the strength that I need to remain strong

Push me towards your love and pull me away from anything wrong

Supply my body with the nutrients which it needs

Allow me to make a difference by planting good seeds

Let every place which I enter into be filled with the spirit of peace

And any evil that come up against me, I ask it to be cease

This is the daily prayer which I pray

To get me through another safe and productive day

Every day above ground is a win

We're all given 24 hours so value how your time is spent

Sheena Johnson   Jewel Dropper

My Sisters

Loud and clear with no whisper, I'm speaking directly to my Sisters

This includes the ones wearing a strap on playing a role of a Mister

Love is Love don't judge, if you see her with her Lady and she kiss her

You can't call someone lifestyle dirty when there's toxins in your filter

Save your tender legal

Free food for thought let me feed you

With a weapon that is lethal

Reincarnated in the 80's to continue the sequel

I'm not a racist, I accept all walks of life as long as their real people

Nothing personal but what's happening to my people

Light Skin and Dark Skin we are all equal

Never think you're better just because your skin tone is fair

Strip yourself bare

Sheena Johnson   Jewel Dropper

Look into the mirror and stare

Accept yourself and save the good if it's any left there

I admire and accept the art of a good weave whether it's short or down to the rear

But never hide and get lost under the hair which you wear

 Your skin, features and natural hair texture is the proof

We're Black and that's the truth

Never disrespect or forget your roots

First, you must show respect to The Master

Then, fully love yourself after

When you know who you are and love who you are your success will grow faster

Sheena Johnson — Jewel Dropper

Runner

Old heads taught me, when falling in love move at a slow pace

Give your mate their space and don't ever chase

But this love shit got me running like I'm in a race

The finish line is near

So, hear me loud and clear

If you don't want me let me know and I'll disappear

They say good love is hard to find

Do you know there's a shortage of great Woman of my kind

A beautiful mind who's loyal and kind plus she stays on her grind

Tell me am I asking for too much

When I want to feel the comfort of your touch

I'll rather have you instead of my favorite hobby, burning loud out of a vanilla dutch

Do you suggest I move on to the next

Do you want the same flex I put on for my ex

Easy come easy go let me know so, I can no longer call you or text

Sheena Johnson   Jewel Dropper

Hood Anthem

Heartache and pain formed had me in rare form when I got dissed

Dr. Jada healed the heartache and pain through The Last Kiss

I'm the author the poet who words move so swift

I go hard on the first, second and graveyard shift

The gift fully equipped it flows between the cleft

I do it for the hood that no longer exist

Mr.Sam, Shawn, Sterling, Donyetta, Netta, Ebony, Krazy D, Peanut, Triple C, Prissy, C-Love, Saadiq, Mookie and Eddie

Ms. Brenda, Ms. Bell, Roc Bird, Ray, Melly Mel, Janyll, Nell, Darnell, Winfield, Hingie, Wannie, Tiffany, Wanya, Desiree, Kenny and Shelly

Pete, Wez, Wheat, Man-Man, Sugarman, Powman, Braheem, Kareem, Haines, Enalla, Junior, Oscar, E and Sun

Sun's life was taking by the gun

A few months before the birth of his son

Kianna, Taquana, Tierra, Asia, Esha, Kineesha, Shaqueena, Ms.B, Ivry and Coco

Sheena Johnson   Jewel Dropper

RonG, EB and The Twins, Kerby, Bobby, Keith, Cruz, Curt, Carlton, Jorge, Sergio, Tito, Juitio, Antonio and Mario

Only Heaven knows why you had to go

Crystal, Troy, Marcus, Kim, Cedric, Duba, Izzy, Tyree, Lori, Terron, Baby Quran, Sharon, Kim, Quan, Ms. Robin, Twain, Mere Anderson's Mom, Capone, Jerome, Jamone and Tone Tone

Enjoy the afterlife of Paradise as you sit on your throne

Along with Ms.Choice, Angie, Tye, Dave, Antoine, Medina, Papa, Cloudy, DC, KC, Reem, Black Moe, Mike-Mike, CoCo, Boof, Grandpop, Granny, Pinky, Uncle Meaty, Mart, Rachel and Willie

Riding their dirt bikes on heaven highways saluting Darrin, Wayne-Wayne and Denny from Philly

Rest in power Ms.Honey, Tank, Uncle Frank, Bismisallah, Dawny, Tommy, Lil E, Dre, Baby J, Sug, Baby A, Jihad, Veezy, Dre, Country, Smitty, Uncle B, Gail, Dee-Dee, Ms. Betsy and T-Nasty

All of you are remembered by being cool, real, chilled, wild, crazy, highly respected, fly, one of a kind or classy

Few cause of their deaths were motor vehicle, suicide and others were from a natural cause

Most of the deaths were murders but those murders are **NONE OF MY BUSINESS** I'm just honoring the lives lost

Continue to rest in Paradise Latif, Ms. Essie, Ms. Jackie, Ms. Anna Mae, Mitch, Yummy, Booda, Lolita, King, Granny and Boss Hoff

Sheena Johnson — Jewel Dropper

Although you're gone, I'm gonna make sure that you're never forgotten

As long as my veins pumps the blood of a Johnson

I gotta keep it pushing ain't no time to be stopping

I stay high and fried always fly with a heel or a sneaker

I'm the instructor, the Professor, the Teacher, the Motivational Speaker

Now a days you can't trust The Priest, The Bishop, The Pastor or The Preacher

No time to be chasing Men I'm too busy chasing paper

A thorough breed that bakes bread better than the baker

My swag comes naturally I'm a Hustler by nature

God's child protected by my Angels wings

The Hood love me Pimps, Whores, Hustlers, Elders, Children and Fiends

The Gang- Bangers, Teenagers, Store Owners and Kings

Sheena Johnson   Jewel Dropper

Real Ones

My rage of being broke is spiraling out of control

I'm young but my soul feels old

As if I was a Senior Citizen or Elderly

Accepting what I can't change through the prayer of Serenity

Ocean deep describes my mentality

Many judging me because their negative energy doesn't balance out with my personality

Hating me but at the same time loving me

The hell with you if your realness

Is occasional like Christmas

I keep all frauds at a distance

Fraud Characters are clones who souls are just an invention

When one of their kind dies I never cry because their existence

 Never made a difference

Trained to go riding solo, don't need a large crown or a team

Sheena Johnson Jewel Dropper

I accept all wisdom given even if it's coming from a cocaine smoking fiend

Murder only hurts when a innocent or real individual is the victim at the scene

If you're not real I don't deal, even if we share the same blood stream

And carry the same gene

Sheena Johnson   Jewel Dropper

The Cage

Two silver tone cuffs cuffed around his ankles and wrists

Someone called the tip hotline and they snitched

A window gated bus transports him while he's on his trip

Freedom is all he'll ask for if he was granted one wish

He made the casual and plain appear sophisticated and nice

His eye focused on the style never the price

Upgraded the mistress as well as the wife

Tossing the homemade soap curved dice

Thinking about those lucky Casino nights

Playing in the game consequences comes with a costly price

Shedding blood, sweat and tears with no fears just sacrifice

Trapped inside a pit can't do shit but exercise

Whenever he enters into a room his presents expresses strength with the power of love

Any Woman or Child will feel safe when embraced by one of his hugs

Purchased drugs by the weight of Bricks and Pounds forming dimes into dubs

Placing it into the hands of a young thug

Sheena Johnson   Jewel Dropper

A snitch is a wishy-washy nigga washed up with no suds

Me, Myself and I am unplugged

Bosses pay attention to your Hustlers because their out here bugged

They're yelling and telling

The same ones who are selling

Giving names with full spellings

When a snitch falls into a ditch the streets become un-wailing

Dishonorable was the cause of the failing

Sorry that their hand got the bad dealing

Charge after charge no Mastercard or Visa

Mentally perplex wondering who's sexing his wifey Lisa

Out of sight & out of mind to his Mistress Theresa

She's on to the next one, told him "I no longer need you"

All he was to her was just a preview

This world is cold and evil

Never bite the hand that feeds you

I consider him a Hustler society considers him a crook

Just the other day he was a Millionaire now today there's no commissary on his books

Sheena Johnson   Jewel Dropper

In a place where it ain't safe, inhaling polluted air that stink, loud noise can't think, through it all facial expression is stuck on one look

Like back the Fuck up before you get hook and you ain't gotta be shook

Respect, I give that so, if not received back then it gotta get took

Several years in

Wishing he can escape his skin

Now realizing he's his only friend

Fed the whole city when he was out but the city shows no love now that he's in

I'm a 80's baby who was raised to be loyal to the end

Being disloyal seems to be the style now this is why I never follow the trend

Sheena Johnson   Jewel Dropper

Exposure

Two wrongs don't make a right

What's done in the dark always comes to the light

The exposure surfaces bright

When you walk righteous, The Creator will reveal all negativity *to your sight*

Keep your radar on The Player playing both sides of the fence

Love doesn't start from your heart it starts with common sense

In my own defense

I'm only sharing this from my own experience

Holding on to one who doesn't want to be held on to is a major hinderance

When identifying Love and Lust you must decipher the difference

A lie is a lie, the truth is the Truth

If love is no longer there, don't make an excuse

Your best bet is to cut it loose

Sticking around being hurt only causes the pain to overproduce

Sheena Johnson — Jewel Dropper

Katrina

Trying to keep their heads above the waters

Mothers and Fathers separated from Sons and Daughters

Instead of bringing in food and water

They brought in cameras and reporters

Broadcasting this devastation on every station

Animals, Babies, Old men and Ladies died from dehydration

Immediately responded to Tsunami but couldn't save your own nation

Many stranded Blacks, Hispanics and Caucasians

Those people were left for death

Calling them the refugees as if they were apart of the group with Wyclef

I dedicated this poem to victims like Hardy Jackson who watch his wife take her last breath

America are we really free?

Kanye West, Jamie Foxx and Oprah Winfrey I truly agree

With all the statements you stated on national TV

All those who survived the winds and the waves

Were still treated like slaves

Sheena Johnson / Jewel Dropper

Diabetics suffered without insulin for days

Pretty soon, this whole world is crumble and fall

So, whatever your spiritual believe is you better give it your all

Weather you believe in Hinduism, Buddhism, Jesus Christ or Allah

Sheena Johnson Jewel Dropper

Fly Girl

Back in the day during Junior High

The Boys used to tease her as she silently cried

She's now transformed into a beautiful Butterfly

Who's educated, confident, sexy, fly with a good vibe

They called her an ugly Bitch, Weirdo and a Nerd

She was a good girl that never got into a fight but somehow found herself beaten by their words

She's now the shit, naturally thick and didn't have to pay for her curves

The same boys who used to diss her wishing they were with her, it's funny how the tables turns

Her soul's on fire, her inner Beauty shines even brighter

A Phenomenal Woman who's presence speaks louder than Alto singing in a choir

She's a positive beneficial source like calcium, protein and fiber

A major figure who forgives all The Haters that treated her horribly when she was a Minor

Sheena Johnson	Jewel Dropper

Resume'

Age 14 is when I got my first job

I remembered looking down at my pay stub saying "Damn, I got robbed"

"You got your own job now so, pay for your own clothes" The excuse I got from my Mom

Earning my own money supporting my own habit, I start getting bombed

Sophomore year

'Worked in fast food as a cashier

Stacking my little pennies and stealing all my gear

A young girl keeping up with her nails and her hair

After high school, I worked for a temp service as a packer

Brought my first car, hustled hard and became a hacker

When your earnings are low, Its difficult to become a Stacker

Worked in major corporation but still considered the least common factor

Worked in dietary preparing the residents trays

Separating the Regular meals from the Pureed

Worked as a Nurses Aide for a day

Sheena Johnson   Jewel Dropper

I was told if I become certified I'll bring home a nice pay

I respect, salute and applaud every hard working CNA

But I have to earn mines in a different way

That's a tough job that needs to increase what it pays

I got my CDL, drove the public bus also, did telemarketing and housekeeping

Pulling trash, scrubbing, dusting mopping and sweeping

When things got rough at the home front I did a little creeping

The relationship was technically over so I considered it hustling you may consider it cheating

I cared for every child under my care at the Daycare Nursery

I was a waitress, telephone operator, I even worked Security

When all along my real Career was within this poetry

Sheena Johnson / Jewel Dropper

Signing Off

She found out her man from Parkside got a dark side

That usually comes out during the night- time

Pours liquor into his system and then it's showtime

Ass naked with his sideline

Which he fucks part time

Whenever its his side bitches turn

How his Lady is feeling at home isn't his concern

Playing with fire thinking he'll never get to burn

Some consequences are permanent even after the lesson's learned

Slinging his dick to different bitches running reckless, disrespectful and careless

The pussy keeps calling him like a bad habit and he's helpless

He has a Beautiful Woman at home who's loving and precious

Loyal, Sexy with immaculate pussy but now she's become sexless

Ignored, bored, uninterested and disconnected

He slept with so many bitches wondered if he fucked any of them unprotected

Everything glitter ain't gold a lot of these hoes are infected

Sheena Johnson   Jewel Dropper

His Lady is checking out and logging off because she's tired of being disrespected

Sheena Johnson Jewel Dropper

Don't Wanna Sell Crack

Sheltered in a home

Mom is doing it all alone on her own without a job or a spouse

Bills gotta get paid, Siblings need clothes on their backs and food in their mouths

Although she's the head of household I gotta go out here and hustle because there's no Man in the house

I don't wanna sell crack

Looked for many jobs put in many apps

But they never called me back

So, I go to what I know I go back to selling crack

A contestant in this game

Grace, Mercy and Loyalty is what saves me but still I'm trapped in this pain

Got these pink bags and this cocaine

About to put the cane on a dinner plate

Cut it with a razor blade

Sealing the bags up with a big lighter, need a lot of flame

When hustling them rocks on the block

Sheena Johnson   Jewel Dropper

You gotta watch out for fake friends while at the same time watching out for the cops

When intimate with a bitch who ain't your bitch carry two types of protection, a rubber and a burner because these bitches will set you up to get shot

Cameras posted on the polls monitoring the fiends, hustlers, customers and hoes but still the game will never stop

My Mom is looking for a financial blessing so she goes to Church listening to a Decan who doesn't practice what he's preaching to the church folks

Do not fornicate, drink or smoke

Your body is your Temple was his main quote

I laughed at that Nigga because he's a whole joke

I saw him picking up a Hooker right after I sold him coke

Many say my mouth is dirty and needs to be cleaned out with soap

That's not what I need I'm up on my hygiene all I really need is hope

Sheena Johnson

Jewel Dropper

3rd Eye

The revolution will not be televised

Majority of these reality programs are falsified

Watered down with lies

We running out of time

Some feels it's almost over so they don't even try

I can't afford to lose, my vision comes with a luxurious live

Funerals for our youth overpopulates graduations and weddings with husbands and wives

To witness a fair fight is rare because now days their fighting with only guns and knives

Blind folding my face making it impossible to see through my eyes

But through my 3rd eye

I identify, recognize and analyze

My Strength, Knowledge and Wisdom

Is stimulated and formulated through a powerful system

As a child I learned from Mr. Briscoe, Ms. Kim, Mrs. Martin, Nancy Choice and Shirley Chisolm

Born into the hood so without choosing instantly became a victim

Sheena Johnson   Jewel Dropper

Pops wasn't around during my childhood years but I still love him and forgive him

Many Warriors on my squad went to Heaven sometimes I wish that I were with them

Lost so many people to murder and cancer there's two ways that I cope

Praying to The Creator asking for hope

Burning on the earth smoke

Clouds flowing through my lungs, inhaling with a deep throat

Apart of The Creator's selection so I already won the election didn't need a campaign or a vote

It's a jewel dropper whenever you hear something I wrote

I'm just a messenger who's here to produce wisdom through these quotes

Sheena Johnson   Jewel Dropper

Lost Baby Mother

She walks to the corner store with her pajamas on while she's yawning

It's 12 noon but to her it feels like six in the morning

She tells the Hustlers the cops are parked up around the corner but it isn't a sincere warning

She only looked out so they can spark her up because she's broke and it's boring

Weed and bad vibes flows through the atmosphere while her 5 kids are presently there

Corrupted language sowing bad seeds as it pierces through the children's ears

Sad point of it all is that she doesn't even care

Her only concern is sucking a dick in exchange to buy something to wear

She's almost thirty but sounds like a teenager when holding a conversation

A project Hoe, low self- esteem and immature lacking motivation

No Driver's License, no permit, a lazy bitch who hates on the next female with education

Sheena Johnson   Jewel Dropper

She's doesn't care as long as there's welfare she doesn't need a diploma or an occupation

Sheena Johnson Jewel Dropper

Knock Off The User

Overcome your past whether your were used, abused or tortured

Aim towards your future

Without the company of a loser cut off the Moocher

In order to break the curse you must break down barriers

Allow The Creator to be your carrier

Release, dismiss and let go of the scavenger

Energy is everything, good energy will make life merrier

I was born in the struggle but a longevity of poverty for me is just a myth

Money, Power, Respect, the key's within my gift

I'm trying to excel and uplift

What you hear is carried by the currents of air, catch my drift

Sheena Johnson — Jewel Dropper

After the Storm

The storm has finally passed by

Now I finally realize

The grass is so much greener on the other side

The gray and gloomy skies are now cleared

The sound of Thunder I no longer hear

The heavy rains which formed the pain have now disappeared

No longer soaking in sorrow

No longer do I have to beg and barrow

Yesterday I went through the storm to have a better tomorrow

The Sun is shining and beaming

I'm vibrant, luminously glowing and gleaming

I'm so Happy and free it almost feels like I'm dreaming

Sheena Johnson · Jewel Dropper

Wise Guide

The Best gifts in life don't come with a box with a bow

You start to know as you grow

Who's a friend or a foe

Time moves fast as days past in weeks, months, seasons and years

I'm trying to manage to have some sort of advantage while I'm here

Only God I fear and only God I trust

Patience is a virtual so don't rush

Keeping your word makes you a greater woman or man so don't bluff

Employee

Moderate day slavery working for small wages

Routine daily stages

Time to turn the pages

Living pay to check to paycheck, sick of going through theses phases

Letting go of fear and becoming more courageous

My riches is within the gift of these words, quotes and phrases

God given talent so, unto him I give all praises

Must hustle harder and smarter in order to develop changes

Occupation smothering my dreams and moves

If I quit my job what will I lose

Dedicating myself to a job or investing in myself what should I choose

Its time to walk out on faith, my words must be diffused

Spread out across The world, I'm just trying to save another girl from getting used

The road to success doesn't stop at a certain age, you must continue to succeed even after your breakthrough

Sheena Johnson   Jewel Dropper

I refuse to abuse the dreams to excel when I am The Truth

The messenger who was sent to nurture our youth

Sheena Johnson   Jewel Dropper

Never Neglect Yourself

I apologize for leaving you stranded

Putting People, Places and Things before you leaving you abandoned

Neglecting you was never my intentions

I got caught up in nonsense and lost my direction

Neglecting you made me lose all focus

Instead of chasing you I was in the ashtray chasing roaches

Diminishing and wasting time becoming hopeless

A lost soul fading away and I didn't even notice

I'm so sorry I left you stranded in the bottom of the pit

Lost sight of myself because I was caught up in the mix

I must rekindle with you so I'm removing myself from all negative conflicts

Nothing is impossible, there's a solution for everything, if something breaks it can be fixed

I must turn the tables before it gets any worst

All I ever wanted was to be happy and not feel so much hurt

Sheena Johnson   Jewel Dropper

If you don't love yourself, trying to love someone else before loving you will never work

I apologize for leaving you stranded is what I said in the first verse

Me, Myself and I is you; I promise to always put myself first

Sheena Johnson

Jewel Dropper

Stopped Looking

I was looking for Love in all the wrong places

Guess that's why love took me through so many phases

Went through so many chapters, flipped through so many pages

Fooled by the million dollar smile painted on their faces

Side- tracked by good dick and a beautiful image

Fooling around with fools who claimed their love was real when it was just a gimmick

Being with me was a blessing along with a privileged

If someone hurts you once, they'll hurt you twice but u won't hurt me again because we're finished

This love thing isn't working

I gave up looking and soul searching

No more Fucking, sucking and twerking

I must find the exit out of this maze because I'm hurting

I thought his love would be a great assistance but it was just a hinder

Sheena Johnson   Jewel Dropper

So much dirt thrown into my soul its time for a spiritual cleanser

Dropping to my knees asking The Creator to please help me I surrender

Send me someone who's respectful, has a good heart, spiritually strong with a love that's tender

Sheena Johnson

Joy

An incredible charm with a laid back style

Something led me to you was it heaven or your smile

Find myself calling you Daddy although I'm not your child

Pure love has me glowing and growing emotions running wild

You refilled the cup of love just when it went empty

Always catch a good vibe every time you're with me

You are filled with positivity and greatness along with a peaceful energy

Removing all mental stress and anxiety with your aura and serenity

Our Love can change the world, its so strong it can prevent a natural disaster

Real Love is what we share, it's a gift given by The Master

You provide so much happiness with good times and lots of laughter

You are a present to my presence can you be my happily ever after

Sheena Johnson — Jewel Dropper

Dream Lover

A desire so strong only you can fulfill

You keep my flow flowing this natural feeling is real

Your body is a journey that I'll like to explore

I'll give you so much satisfaction you'll be begging for more

You'll never get bored I'll keep you entertained

Every time will be different no time will be the same

Come feel the gentle touch of the softest thing on earth

Sugar walls produce candy drops come feel them as they burst

My pussy has a thick width and deep length, best believe I got that work

I'm also a faithful lover so for you that's a perk

All this love is waiting for you deal or no deal

If you got a Lady there's no way we can build

But if you're Single like myself come and show me something real

Sheena Johnson   Jewel Dropper

Can I Comfort You

Behind your beautiful smile I noticed a frown

Its hurting me to see you look so down

I'll always be around

My comfort will always be near

Have no fear

I'm a friend who will always be here

Men usually don't deal with emotions they usually just cry in the dark

I'm an open ear I'm here for you; you share a special place in my heart

Dealing with the tragedy of your family member passing

Your sister is now in heaven with all the angels classing

So, please don't worry and be depress

I ask God to bring you the strength to overcome your stress

Your Sister is in her heaven living her Best

She wants you to be successful, wealthy, healthy and progress

They say time heals all wounds but truthfully some wounds never heal

No matter what life hits you with, you must remain real

Sheena Johnson — Jewel Dropper

Don't push yourself over the edge just have faith and chill

Allow The Creator to take the wheel

Her death wasn't a downfall

God called her home during his daily role call

She living on a land where there's no hater, manipulators or people who blackball

No sickness, blood pressure issues or high cholesterol

She's happy and free living extraordinary with luxury

In the land of the heavenly

She's with all the other loved ones we lost, keeping each other good company

Sheena Johnson Jewel Dropper

Brainwashed

Hiding and seeking towards ignorance

Now I've become lifeless due to the lack of experience

Captured in bondage for not using my knowledge to allow me to explore

Laziness has become my comfort zone allowing me to never win this self- war

Constantly blaming our roots and society

For our own actions causing an imbalanced personality

Principles and values lost which was once gained

Leaving you with nothing just a fingerprint, SBI number and a name

So much negative energy and confrontation

Due to the fact we're not using our observation and listening techniques because we're too busy involved in meaningless conversation

Thinking our survival kit only consist of food, clothing, shelter and water

There's more like strength, courage, wisdom and order

Establishing plots with an unfinished conclusion

Makes the climax pointless with continuous confusion

If you keep denying yourself for who and what you are

Your achievements will remain at a stand- still allowing you to never get far

Sheena Johnson — Jewel Dropper

Over

Did the strongest girl in the world fall victim to weak

Or did I fall victim to the one I loved with every heartbeat

My lovely warm heart which was warmer than heat

Is now bitter like the middle of winter and hard as concrete

My head aches and my heart burns like an over processed perm

I gave you my loyalty and word but you gave me nothing in return

All along I've should've known

I was nurturing this relationship on my own

When I needed you the most you never picked up your phone

The cat chase the mouse game is never played when you're grown

Thought we had something to build

Your love was never real

 The only thing I was to you, was just another lustful desire fulfilled

Sheena Johnson   Jewel Dropper

Closed Curtain

As of now nothing even matters

My heart is broken into pieces that are scattered

My dreams of loving you for life have shattered

For too many years I've been hurting

The love I've provided was faithfully for certain

The show is over, somebody please shut this motherfucking curtain

Save all your shout outs, standing ovations and applause

Fuck you and your dick that was smaller than your balls

You crossed me like there's no universal laws

Like what goes around comes around always comes back harder

You should've been more smarter

You was thinking with your dick's head instead of thinking with the head under your size 7 ½ size Starter

I'm filled with rage, hurt, pain and anger

Fucking with these nasty whores putting my life in danger

When I see you it's Fuck You, you get treated like a stranger

Sheena Johnson Jewel Dropper

Changing Lanes

We both know things aren't the same

But who do we blame

One another or the game

I'm not feeling the sudden change

Of you acting strange

Pouring out my love and not getting any love in exchange

Losing interest in each others desires

Has us playing with fire

True love never expires

Love is blind

It can make a sane person lose their mind

Viewing comments, likes and emojis reading between the lines

Beginning to ask myself were you ever mine

You've become frustrated by the littlest things

My smile, style, my dreams and the way I wear weaves

I thought you were a perfect King but you were just make believe

Nine out ten plays a fool and a sucker

To that one Motherfucker

Sheena Johnson   Jewel Dropper

That you ALWAYS LOVED but really never was your lover

Sheena Johnson Jewel Dropper

Canceled Program

I loved you genuinely and faithfully

The whole time I was loving you, you were hating me

Your life is too private, it's been years and people barely know your dating me

It's always good in the beginning but nothing last forever

Mixed business with pleasure

Emotions put me under pressure

Dealing with a co-worker who I should've left at the time clock

After we clocked out, I invited you to my spot

And start letting you pop

Sexual Healing brought desire and fire into the Winter

Exchanged body heat, a space heater and opened oven door kept us warm through the blizzard

I played hard to get with other Men so, those other Men are trying to figure how you get her

Kept the pussy juicy when he sucked the toe of the camel

Many episodes through many seasons but this program is now canceled

The show is over, it's time to change the channel

Sheena Johnson   Jewel Dropper

No royalties and No reruns

Maybe if you could've let go of your darken past, you could've been the one

It's obvious you aint the one so You and I are done

Sheena Johnson   Jewel Dropper

The Flip Side

A pleasant and positive Man who makes things happen

Your talk wasn't cheap, you proved it through your actions

Produced intense joy with a deep satisfaction

Eased my emotional and mental state from all negative distractions

An Aries and Gemini forming a vibe unbreakable

He changed up on me now that vibe is unfavorable

A kind Man transformed into the Devil, carrying toxins which are flammable

I am a Woman who will never be forgotten so, never think your unexchangeable

My loyalty never flipped or slipped

I remained loyal and true through the entire relationship

You showed your true colors when you start getting on that disrespectful shit

You were the one I wanted to build with now you're the one I'm about to quit

Sheena Johnson   Jewel Dropper

My Mother's Child

Thoughts about an abortion but without you choosing God chosen you to give birth

Using you as a vessel to deliver me on this earth

Your features are in my face, your blood is in my system

Your struggle is my strength, your knowledge is my wisdom

Taught me that everything in life has a purpose

Also told me to never become hopeless but stay focused

Taught me how to knuckle up, back to the wall whenever at war

If you don't stand for something you'll fall for anything so, know what you stand for

Although, when I was planted my Mother didn't plan it

But life abundantly for me is what The Creator granted

Some of us were born in unstable environments while others were born with the silver spoon

We come from all walks of life and make it many different ways to the Tomb

One thing we all share in common, we came through a Woman's womb

Sheena Johnson   Jewel Dropper

Jezebel

Dirty Diana would let anybody bang her

She'll sleep with her Best Friend's Man she'll even sleep with a stranger

She think she's winning when she's losing, polluted with poison her life is in danger

Everyone knows she's a Hoe, besides God nothing can save her

She'll give it to you raw, anal, vaginal and oral

A Loose Goose never loyal

No values No morals

A spoiled pussy IS DEADLY, it can put you six feet under soil

Heartless, envious and shameless

When the topic of Love is being discussed

She's like change the subject or hush

She'll rather talk about being fucked

Jezebel was once a pure Virgin whose sweet juices became sour

Ladies, our vaginas are our flowers

You must keep it fresh everyday with two or more showers

Sheena Johnson   Jewel Dropper

In my opinion, loyal pussy carries power

Dropping down your underwear, exposing your rear

To a stranger, allowing him to poke you bare

Causes damage to the pussy which causes wear and tear

Instead of damaging your pussy show it tender, love and care

Sheena Johnson   Jewel Dropper

Camelot Troy

A cool Young King that always made me laugh, he had good humor

He said, "Don't believe everything you hear but at the same time don't sleep on a rumor"

His wisdom will make anyone a Happy consumer

He was loved by the Ladies

He made beautiful Babies

He said, "Men respect motivated Women who aren't lazy"

He taught you to embrace your haters

Not with open arms but by becoming Greater

Don't lean or barrow and don't do too many favors

My heart was broken and my nerves were shaken

When I heard this Man's life was taken

A couple days after Troy's death they killed Crazy-D, it was too much to take in

When it came to The Youth he always helped us

Whether we were being good or reckless he always blessed us

With some good bud or life lessons

His earthly years were truly a blessing

Sheena Johnson   Jewel Dropper

Men teaching The Youth is slim on today's market

October 2001 is when a real one had to depart us

He was called home to reunite with his little brother Marcus

Sheena Johnson   Jewel Dropper

Quran Geter

You was here exactly six months December to June

Never thought your precious journey would've ended so soon

We share the same blood, we both grew in the same womb

You're now higher than the stars and moon

I remember visiting you at the hospital the day our Mother gave birth

You were one of the most amazing people to have landed on this earth

I want to ask why but they say you should never question God just put him first

Baby Quran Sameer while you were here your life served a purpose

Life is short that's why you must live positive and stay focus

Could there have been anything done to provoke this

The love I have for Quran is priceless

I wanted to spend more time with you but my visitation got denied by DYFS

Never thought our last visit would've been me viewing you lifeless

Although you didn't live to be one year old

Sheena Johnson   Jewel Dropper

I'm fully aware and understand that God is in control

Live life by keeping your word and Never bend or fold

Sheena Johnson　　　　　　　　　　　　　　　　Jewel Dropper

I Need Growth

Time to change the route

Hydrate the drought

Water the seed in the concrete so the rose can sprout

No need to argue or shout

Its done up, the box (pussy) is closed, locked down and shut

I love you but not the energy you bring to me so you gotta get cut

The universe gives what you need and also gives you what you want

Always be present, true to your word and never front

Demons are out here like a Marshall on a manhunt

Stealing, Killing and violating people's lives

We all have demons whether its through drugs, gambling, drinking or having high sex drives

The best way to stay protected is through prayer, being aware and positive vibes

I enjoyed what we had

The good and the bad

However, being stagnated without growth subtracts and never adds

Sheena Johnson   Jewel Dropper

Being Set Free

Similar to a phone call with bad service we broke up

If you knew you didn't want me from the start you should've spoke up

We're the same age but not on the same page because you refuse to grow up

You disgust me just like throw up when you said you had to give up

It took my breath away like a hiccup

Pulled me up to push me down like a sit up

All this wasted time held me up like a stick up

You told me to spread my pretty wings and fly

I couldn't understand why

At this point I can no longer try

So, I'm cutting all tides

I would be saying a boldface lie

If I said the departure didn't make me cry

But now those tears have dried

Like laundry on a clothesline

Self- esteem has been increased and self- love has been redefined

Sheena Johnson   Jewel Dropper

A Monster Without a Face

For many years there's been lots of questions left unanswered

If I had one wish It'll be to come up with a cure for all Cancer

I'm not referring to the zodiac sign from the end of June into mid July

I am referring to the deadly disease that causes millions to lose their lives

Many patients experience Chemotherapy, intake many meds and experience treatments such as the Gamme knife

This Monster can attack your Pets, Mother, Father, Brother, Sister, Aunt, Uncle, Cousin, Husband or Wife

It can appear in your prostate, ovaries, breast, blood and inside of your throat

It can appear in your lungs even if you've never smoked

A mass murderer without a face

The world is too focused on what's in space

Instead of finding solutions for the problems here at The home base

If there's a cure, please release the formula and information from your lab and database

It's bullying the bodies of the babies, it's such a disgrace

Sheena Johnson   Jewel Dropper

I salute every Pediatric Doctor and Nurse who goes above and beyond to put a smile on their patients faces

Making the environment of their hospital stay a magical Oasis

Cancer is an unwelcome intruder, intruding people's lives on the daily basis

It doesn't matter if your black or white, this disease isn't racist

When Rapper Nasir Jones lost his Mother you can feel his pain when you hear "If heaven was a mile away" one of the strongest songs on my playlist

Cancer is even more scary,

 When the disease is hereditary

Cherish and Love your loved ones, not just on the 14th of February

The World is getting crazier every day and it's scary

To everyone who's lost someone and cancer was the cause

 I know what you're going through and I'm sorry for your lost

Sheena Johnson   Jewel Dropper

Janyll Burley

I'm so hurt I don't know how to start

We met in the early 90's in Ivy Hills at the park

Showed me your straight A report card which proved you were smart

Your strength stronger than a Gladiator

You never ever was a hater

More like a congratulator and motivator

Swag stayed on a hundred weather you was rocking a Jordan or a Gator

76ers was her favorite team, basketball's her favorite sport

If you were loyal to her, she gave it back with a strong force

Never put yourself second, third or fourth; put yourself first is something she enforced

Imported from Heaven on October 29, 1986

Janyll aka Jessie you're truly missed

She was called back home on March 02, 2006

She never was a troublemaker but when trouble will come to her she was nice with her fist

Sheena Johnson   Jewel Dropper

She loved good food, nature, animals and kids

Whenever any of her Homies got locked up she'll support them through their bids

A person who loved to give

Never selfish or Greedy

Always fed the hungry and gave to the needy

The realist Rocafella fan who loved Shawn Carter, Young Gunz, Memphis Bleek, Freeway, Petey and Beanie

Many people with the name Janyll but you was one of a kind

A nineteen years young Leader with a wise mind

Last thing she said to me, "If I should die don't cry"

Find the Best Herb and get high

Man can't heal me only God can heal me, if it's my time it's my time

We all gotta number so live, love, teach and learn

She wasn't afraid of anything , she was dying from Cancer and death wasn't her concern

She said," I did good deeds on this earth so, I know my soul won't burn"

Be all you were sent here to be before it's your turn

Signals

My mind signals a yellow light to proceed with caution and take it slow

My heart flashes a red light to stop while my body signals a green light to go

It's your call, you can have it all

The Creator used you to build me up so please don't let me fall

Your irreplaceable love is so enticing

You can have your cake and eat it too, whipped cream cherry on top of the icing

Provided an abundance of Ambition like Wale's sophomore album

I was already focused but out of no where you came through and pumped up the volume

When his head's high, I kill him with a blow

Swerving K-Turns, U-Turns and Donuts on the pole as I ride him like a Pro

A loyal Queen who throws that thing back with that comeback

A Man can only get full off of a meal not just a snack

A Phenomenal Woman that's never intimidated by those other girls

Sheena Johnson   Jewel Dropper

My only concern is that you continue to bring joy into my world

I was once doubtful and indecisive but now I'm fully confident

You leave me with a fruitful energy so powerful and dominant

Sheena Johnson   Jewel Dropper

Never Make It More

Old Heads be careful when dealing with the legal age young boy who you toy

Never make it more than what it is claiming it's Love and Joy

When it can't fill the void

Purchasing his boxers, socks, tees, pants, shirts, sneaks, hoodies, coats and jackets

She supports his kids, liquor and drug habit

The money that she gives him, he spends on the girls in his age bracket

Washed up Old Head whose priorities needs to be straighten

Her soul remains vacant

Got her raising hell like flames decorated in the home of Satan

Young Boy giving her hell, making her go on a rampage

High mileage on the pussy makes her unwanted by the Men her age

Everything ain't for everybody but this one posts everything on her page

We're all human, we all get in a sexual mood

It's not good to let everyone see you in the nude

Sheena Johnson   Jewel Dropper

Everybody ain't suppose to poke the pussy, some sex you gotta exclude

Once upon a time she used to be the shit, the kids now days would've called her lit

Bad karma and bad pussy is what you'll get, when u let everybody hit

Young ladies this is truth and not dare

Live life just make sure your playing it safe out here

Every Man isn't suppose to see you face down with your ass in the air

Your pussy is a precious power; preserve it from becoming wear and tear

Sheena Johnson   Jewel Dropper

The Way You Love Me

I love it when you please me

Hold me, touch me and tease me

When we make love I love when you move and squeeze me

I must confess thee

You please me

When you caress me

Sweet milk chocolate body that's sweeter than nestle

You give my soul joy and energy

You take my mind to Africa, India and Italy

When I wasn't on my "A" game you never looked at me differently

Although, I'm living in poverty your love makes me feel rich

You never physically or mentally hurt me or ever called me a Bitch

That's why I'm holding on tightly like an open wound does to a stitch

You woke me up when I was dozing

That's why I tell all others I'm chosen

This affair that we share is rare so please lets keep it frozen

Sheena Johnson — Jewel Dropper

Cardiac Care

I loved him with all of my heart I swear

My heart is so damaged it needs prayer

Along with cardiac care

He was my everything now without him I'm bare

Fully cloth feeling ass naked

Thought our bond connected

Slid lust demons inside of me each time my pussy got injected

An exchange that I can't change so I gotta accept it

No matter how good it is to my pussy, my soul says no so, I gotta reject it

I proudly take the blame for becoming neglected

Hurt by the one I elected

I put my vote in his ballot, he's the one I selected

Our course of Chemistry

Is now a course of History

Can't keep trying to solve your mystery

Dropping a bad habit is hard to let go, temptation is dangerous when accompanied by an addictive energy

Sheena Johnson   Jewel Dropper

Dope Addict

I'm going crazy, strung out like a fiend

This Bad Girl needs her ass beat so, go get the belt while I'll pull down my jeans

The high off of a dope dick feels like a sweet dream

Slip, sliding, colliding, riding, sucking and cuffing while we're fucking

One hit of The Dope Dick got me bugging

The type of high you can't share with a cousin

The only drug that numbs all my pain

As it flows through my veins

Poking needles under my skin, forever wearing your name

It's always on command when he gives his orders

Putting that thing far back in my throat until my eyes water

Whenever life throws a heavy luggage, the drug takes the weight off like a Porter

You got me "Feenin" like Jodeci

Diary of a Mad Band album 93'

I tried leaving The Pipe alone but The Pipe keeps calling me

Sheena Johnson   Jewel Dropper

Closure

I see you've become bored

My feelings have faded because when they were existing they were ignored

I guarantee my pussy is better than any Bitch you whored

Pussy's juicy and tight like a virgin

When I'm twerking I put that work in

Like an illegal immigrant does while their working

You had me all to yourself

I never fucked no one else

Now I'm back on the market because you placed me on the shelve

Hurt and pain got me stressing

Being approached and second guessing

This was just a valuable lesson to always pay attention

A man can fuck with a quiet sneaky hoe

Thinking no one will ever know

What's done in the dark always shines bright like a light show

When a person's words doesn't match their actions

 You must cut off the attachment

Sheena Johnson   Jewel Dropper

Fraudulent behavior was the cause of the detachment

Cleansing my soul of all elements which are filthy

Putting restraints on all evil things that temps me

It's time to furnish the spaces in my spirit that are empty

Sheena Johnson   Jewel Dropper

I'm Up

When you sleep you get slept on I had to wake up from my nap

I tried hard to avoid the legal age young boy but one fell into my lap

My earthly years compared to his are greater by a five year gap

Held him up because I cared for him but in return he didn't have my back

Never bite the hand that feeds you

You'll need me in some form of fashion way before I'll ever need you

What you put out you'll pull in

This will happen again

When you meet if you haven't already met that special friend

A love so sweet you'll fall deep then it will suddenly end

I'm far from the hater type

Got played took it to the chin, kept it pushing on some humble shit no need in getting hype

I applaud the universal law "What goes around comes around" one of the major facts of life

It wasn't in my plans to love and assist this young Man but all things happen for a reason

Sheena Johnson   Jewel Dropper

Added light to your life when I sowed and planted good seeds through good deeds, I was only trying to show you something decent

Lights out

It's a black out

You're faded out

Invisible into the current season

Sheena Johnson — Jewel Dropper

Turn The Tables

Life is what you make it

If there's a generational curse in your bloodline, be the one to break it

Try not to duplicate it or trace it

Attend to yourself and your kids before giving someone else all your attention

If you're an employee and your employer is causing you tension

Stay humble for that 401K, health care and pension

Remember, being disrespected isn't listed in your job description

Working under a coward in power makes one go harder on their mission

Using this labor to give birth to my dreams and visions

Up and coming to you live

An OG giving wisdom with no bribe

Never let life end at your failures; learning while your living makes you wise

Never give your emotions more muscle than you give your mind

Always be your best & stay focus on the grind

Sheena Johnson   Jewel Dropper

Fast Pace

Lift every voice and sing

Til' earth and heaven ring

Was my favorite song back in Elementary

Unfortunately, it was only played in the month of February

That song gave me more hope than hearing my teachers say, "Be All You Can Be"

Children enjoy your childhood and don't live life in a hurry

If so, you'll prematurely age yourself with too much drugs, sex, liquor and worry

You are going to be older longer than you're going to be younger so, don't live your childhood wastefully

Stay in your lane and NEVER be a hater, this way you'll age gracefully

Children don't rush your life because in life somethings need time to grow

Mind your business, drink your water and avoid becoming a sucker or a hoe

Sheena Johnson · Jewel Dropper

Long Distance Lover

Conversated and Chilled

When I let him inside the box, he delivered a satisfying thrill

The law of attraction, especially sexual attraction is real

You came to me out of the blue

Time flew and feelings grew

Who would've known I would've hook up with you

Hardships became involved

Anger and arguments evolved

Many years, tears, pain and problems left unsolved

Barely sexing or texting too busy out here flexing, tell me where is the love

Hardly speaking, no greets or hugs

I hate what we've become it's nothing like it was

It's always good in the beginning

Somehow all that greatness went missing

Our lips are no longer kissing

Because our mouths are full of name calling and dissing

Never honoring each other existence

Sheena Johnson   Jewel Dropper

How is our love long distance

When we both reside under the same residence

We're unequally yoked, its evident

Sheena Johnson · Jewel Dropper

Halfway House

Two full time jobs working crazy ass shifts

Didn't really have the time for you but I sacrificed and made a fit

Put heavy mileage on the whip

I did what you demanded and never gave you no lip

Treated him like a King as if he was my legal spouse

When we never exchange vows in a Chapel or inside of a courthouse

There's nothing left to reconstruct once damage strikes inside of the glasshouse

Experienced restless nights when I accommodated him when he was a resident in the halfway house

I always came through with those home cooked platters

During that Travel Time, gave him a fat pussy with sweet juices that splattered

His lies and bull shit has me unflatter

Due to his bull shit, my dreams of love have shattered

Thought what we had was fond

Your words weren't attached with a bond

I never let anyone else dive in your pond

Sheena Johnson   Jewel Dropper

Once The King got released and landed on these streets

The life of our love instantly deceased

This relationship is killing me slowly like a deadly disease

We both must keep it cordial and respect each other's peace

We both respect each other's credit, we can't break the lease

Until we go our separate ways

We'll remain friends and hopefully we'll have better days

I'll rather be celibate & single, Men aren't serious all they wanna do is play

Sheena Johnson   Jewel Dropper

The Pussy Chase

Excuse me if I sound rude as I get specific

Don't mean to toot my own horn but my pussy is terrific

Wetter and deeper than The Marianna Trench ocean beneath the Western Pacific

No matter how good the pussy is made, Men are always going to crave for something different

You can own the best vagina on the planet

Made of sweet juices of pomegranate

He can still love you but take you for granted

Under a spell of these filthy soul Bitches

 Demons and negative energies forming intermixes

From his point of view, their just easy fixes

Jeopardizing his solid rock at home for a few sucks, strokes and body liquids

If you cheat, pick out a side chick that doesn't cheat

We'll never beef or compete

We can all come to the same table and eat

Sheena Johnson   Jewel Dropper

Would I be breaking tradition or considered weird if I tell her to pull up a chair

For most Men, fucking with one Woman is like not having air
More Bitches more pussy keeps his airwaves clear

Sheena Johnson — Jewel Dropper

The Good Die Young

His Mother is crying asking why did my baby have to go

Neighbors saying he was a good child I watched him grow

Fake Friends wearing airbrush shirts which displays "In Loving Memory of a Real Nigga"

Attending the Funeral as if they're not the ones who pulled the trigger

His little Sister is only two years old so, she doesn't really know what's going on

All she thinks that her Brother is sleep when he's really gone

He lays in all white linen with flowers and roses lying beside his death bed

His Grandparents dressed in all black saying he should've listen to what we said

His Cousin is up State in a cell going through hell, he just received the bad news

Looking down at the obituary his biological Father is crying because being involved in his son's life is what he abused

Sheena Johnson   Jewel Dropper

His Aunt is crying tears of pain asking God to bring her nephew back

A young Boss who had older individuals asking if they can trap

He was only a teen living the street dream, focused on the green

Humble and loyal, he never disrespected anyone not even a fiend

A young guy who had no fear

So young that he just started growing a beard

A heart of a lion

He brought joy to the world like Lauryn Hill's Zion

I once saw a quote saying "Your Biggest Hater is never a stranger"

He was loyal to the wrong friends which put him in danger

His oldest Brother is hurt preparing for war yet he shows no anger

When a person is mad but calm

A fortuneteller can't predict there next move even if they read their palm

The shooters are at the funeral paying their fake condolence unaware their bodies are the next to get embalmed

Life after death

His girlfriend is pregnant with his child, The Creator knows best

A great soul lasts forever, even after the body takes its last breath

Jewels

Life is too short to be walking around with a bad attitude

It weakens your mental health whenever your mean and rude

Try not to feud

Never expect success if your slothful and sluggish

If you hear something real listen and try not to change the subject

Love yourself and discard the opinions of the public

Never ignore the intuition that sits within your stomach

Just because I'm humble and amongst the meekest

Never take my kindness as a weakness

If you cross me, in exchange I'll hit you with a rage that'll leave you speechless

Sheena Johnson Jewel Dropper

Icy Cold World

The human race

Has become a disgrace

Judging based upon personality, sexuality and race

Surf on a positive wave in exchange The Universe will bring u good karma

All Blacks aren't bad people, tell me where do they come up with this drama

Cops whole purpose is to serve and protect

Why are they offing my people with bullets, chokeholds and knees pressed against necks

Everyday I pray for world peace

Seems like the more I pray the more the violence increase

Out here living just keeping my soul on a clean streak

Why is love such a hard battle to fight

It doesn't matter if your black or white

Is what we was told by Mike

We are a human race

Sheena Johnson

Jewel Dropper

Divided with lost faith

It's time we love one another, hate is a disgrace

All Officers aren't bad, Fuck the bad ones who's racist

Killing innocent Minorities on a daily basis

To all the humans, birds, bees and trees

We all need the same air and oxygen to breath

World peace and prosperity is what I ask for when I'm down on bending knees

I'm so sick of seeing so many Mothers grieve

I'm just trying to make a flip

By making spirits lift

Through this wisdom being spoken out of this cleft lip

Acknowledgments

All honor and praise to The Creator, through you all things are possible. I thank you for giving me the gift of poetry. Grandma, thanks for the wisdom and strength you installed in me. Moe, thanks for always being a real one. You always stayed true and never switched up. I'm thankful to have you. Tye Mease, I appreciate the endless support you've given to me. To everyone that remained loyal to me, I thank you wholeheartedly. Loyalty is a treasured gift. To all my friends and family, thanks for the love and support. Mrs. Martin, you gave me such inspiration and hope as a young child. You were always honest and caring. I thank God for you. To every reader who have read this book, may my talent serve you in a positive way. Everyday above ground is a win.

I dedicate this book to Granny, Janyll, King, Bismillah and Brian. You are forever in my heart.

Sheena JohnsonJewel Dropper

Order form

Print name

Address

City

Phone

State

Zip

Sheena Johnson

P.O. Box 114

Lawnside, N.J. 08045

@s.jewel_dropper

	Date	Quantity	Quality
Jewel Dropper			

Sheena Johnson Jewel Dropper

Sheena Johnson   Jewel Dropper

www.ingramcontent.com/pod-product-compliance
Lightning Source LLC
Chambersburg PA
CBHW060836050426
42453CB00008B/721